BLESSED NAMES
Why Was He Named al-Mahdi (AJ)?

Written by:
Kisa Kids Publications

Please recite a Fātiḥah for the marḥūmīn
of the Rangwala family, the sponsors of this book.

All proceeds from the sale of this book
will be used to produce more educational resources.

Dedication

This book is dedicated to the beloved Imām of our time (AJ). May Allāh (swt) hasten his reappearance and help u
become his true companions.

Acknowledgements

Prophet Muḥammad (s): The pen of a writer is mightier than the blood of a martyr.

True reward lies with Allāh, but we would like to sincerely thank Shaykh Salim Yusufali and Sisters Sabika Mith
Liliana Villalvazo, Zahra Sabur, Kisae Nazar, Sarah Assaf, Nadia Dossani, Fatima Hussain, Naseem Rangwala, a
Zehra Abbas. We would especially like to thank Nainava Publications for their contributions. May Allāh bless them
this world and the next.

Preface

*Prophet Muḥammad (s): Nurture and raise your children in the best way. Raise them with the love of the Proph
and the Ahl al-Bayt (a).*

Literature is an influential form of media that often shapes the thoughts and views of an entire generation. Therefc
in order to establish an Islamic foundation for the future generations, there is a dire need for compelling Islar
literature. Over the past several years, this need has become increasingly prevalent throughout Islamic centers a
schools everywhere. Due to the growing dissonance between parents, children, society, and the teachings of Isl
and the Ahl al-Bayt (a), this need has become even more pressing. Al-Kisa Foundation, along with its subsidia
Kisa Kids Publications, was conceived in an effort to help bridge this gap with the guidance of ʿulamah and the help
educators. We would like to make this a communal effort and platform. Therefore, we sincerely welcome construct
feedback and help in any capacity.

The goal of the *Blessed Names* series is to help children form a lasting bond with the 14 Māʿṣūmīn by learni
about and connecting with their names. We hope that you and your children enjoy these books and use them a:
means to achieve this goal, inshā'Allāh. We pray to Allāh to give us the strength and tawfīq to perform our duties a
responsibilities.

With Duʾās,
Nabi R. Mir (Abidi)

Kisa Kids Publications
4415 Fortran Court
San Jose, CA 95134
(260) KISA-KID [547-2543]

An Introduction to the Blessed Names

Our names are a very special part of us. Many times, they shape our personalities and even explain who we are or the person we would like to become. In this series, you will explore the names and titles of our beloved 14 Ma'soomeen. Did you know that their names and titles were not just ordinary names? They were special because they were given to them by Allah!

Allah has given seven special heavenly names to our Ma'soomeen: Muhammad, Ali, Fatimah, Hasan, Husain, Ja'far, and Musa. Behind each of these names is a heavenly power!

In addition to their names, each of the Ma'soomeen also had special titles by which they became famous. Their titles were often given to them because of the circumstances of their time, but these titles and characteristics were common amongst all the Ma'soomeen. For example, Imam al-Baqir (a) was known for spreading knowledge because he was able to create many new universities and branches of knowledge during his time. However, if the other Ma'soomeen had the same opportunity, they, too, would have spread knowledge and created universities in their teaching circles. In these stories, you will discover some of the reasons why the Ma'soomeen received their specific names or titles.

Many of us share our names with these beloved Ma'soomeen or know people who do. Let's learn about these blessed names and titles so we can strive to be like our blessed Ma'soomeen!

I think al-Mahdi means...

_____

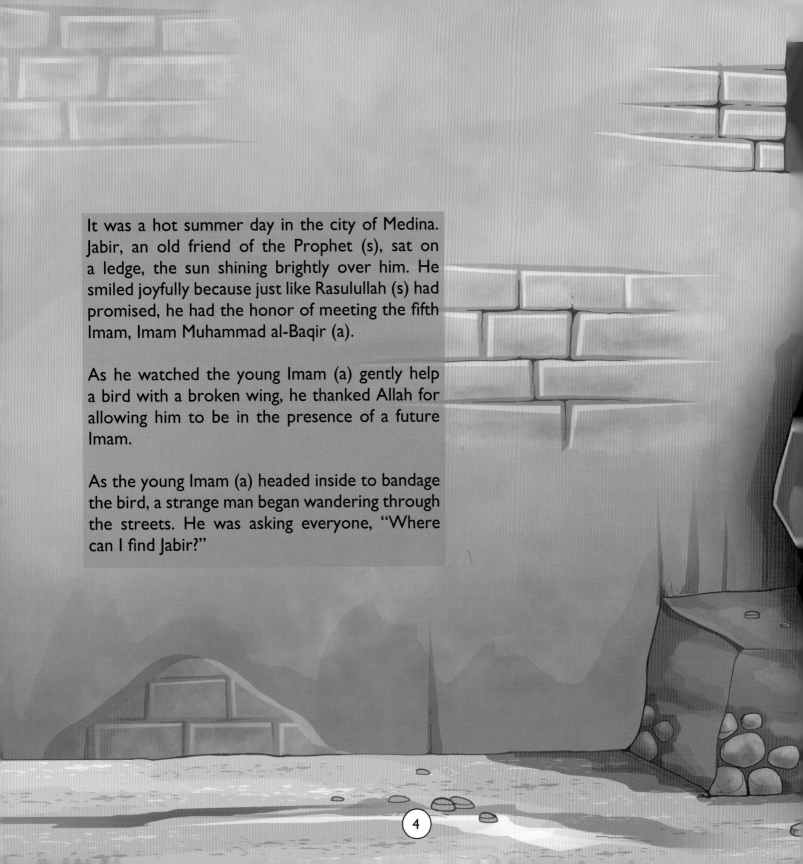

It was a hot summer day in the city of Medina. Jabir, an old friend of the Prophet (s), sat on a ledge, the sun shining brightly over him. He smiled joyfully because just like Rasulullah (s) had promised, he had the honor of meeting the fifth Imam, Imam Muhammad al-Baqir (a).

As he watched the young Imam (a) gently help a bird with a broken wing, he thanked Allah for allowing him to be in the presence of a future Imam.

As the young Imam (a) headed inside to bandage the bird, a strange man began wandering through the streets. He was asking everyone, "Where can I find Jabir?"

The villagers led the man to the house of Imam as-Sajjad (a), where Jabir was sitting outside. He quickly walked up to Jabir and greeted him "Salaamun Alaikum!"

Jabir replied, "Wa Alaikum Salaam," and watched as the mysterious man tried to catch his breath.

The man said, "Dear Jabir, I have been searching for you all over the city! I have so many questions, and I was told you are a knowledgeable companion of the Prophet (s) and Imams (a)."

Jabir happily answered as many questions as he could, using the knowledge he had gained from the Prophet (s) and the Imams (a). Finally, the man asked a question to which Jabir didn't know the answer!

The curious man asked, "Why is the last Imam (AJ) named 'al-Mahdi?'"

As Jabir pondered over this question, the man spotted the young Imam al-Baqir (a) coming back out of his home. Both he and Jabir rushed to the Imam (a) and gave him their salaam.

Jabir and the man knew this was a good opportunity to get their question answered, so the man again asked, "O my Imam (a), why will the last Imam (AJ) be given the title 'al-Mahdi?'"

Imam al-Baqir (a) smiled and answered, "He will be named 'al-Mahdi,' meaning 'the one who is guided by Allah.' He will use his guidance to guide people, even during times when no one will be able to see him. His presence with be like the sun's, which shines even when it is hidden behind the clouds."

The man found this answer to be very interesting.

The Imam (a) continued, "He will bring out the original heavenly books from a cave and guide people of each religion through their own books: the Jews through the Torah, the Christians through the Bible, and the Muslims through the Quran."

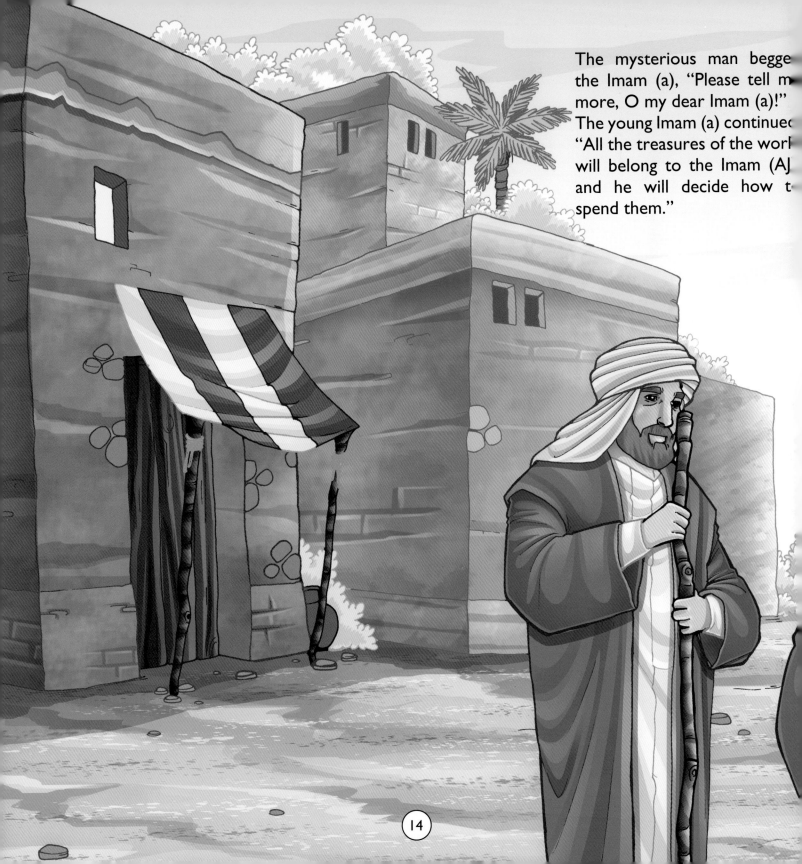

The mysterious man begge[d] the Imam (a), "Please tell m[e] more, O my dear Imam (a)!" The young Imam (a) continued[:] "All the treasures of the worl[d] will belong to the Imam (AJ[)] and he will decide how t[o] spend them."

The man was now bursting with love for Imam al-Mahdi (AJ) and so he pleaded, "My knowledge is so limited! Please tell me more about my beloved Imam al-Mahdi (AJ)!"

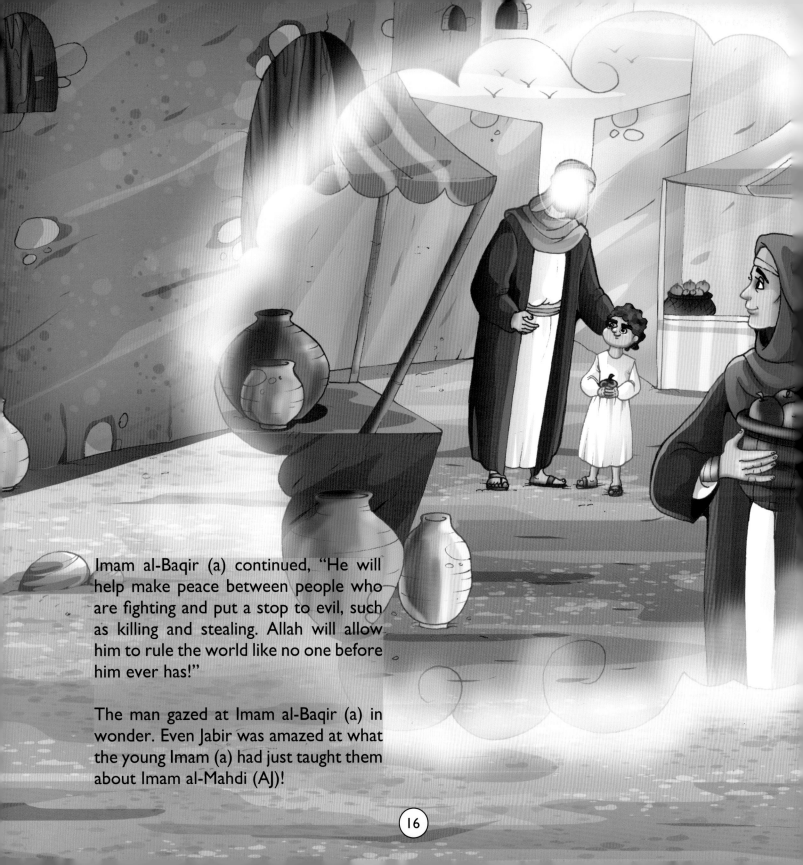

Imam al-Baqir (a) continued, "He will help make peace between people who are fighting and put a stop to evil, such as killing and stealing. Allah will allow him to rule the world like no one before him ever has!"

The man gazed at Imam al-Baqir (a) in wonder. Even Jabir was amazed at what the young Imam (a) had just taught them about Imam al-Mahdi (AJ)!

The mysterious man had finally found the answers to his questions and thanked the young Imam (a). He bowed down and kissed the Imam's hand out of respect. He also thanked Jabir for answering all his previous questions. The man politely bid farewell to the Imam (a) and Jabir, then disappeared into the busy streets of the city.

Jabir thought hard about what he had learned from Imam al-Baqir (a). He felt overjoyed to have learned all this new information.

As Jabir sat back down, he smiled at the shining face of Imam al-Baqir (a).

Many years ago, Jabir used to go to the Prophet (s) whenever he had any questions. He was so thankful to Allah that he had lived to meet *five* Imams after him from whom he was also able to learn so much!

Nobody in all of Medina had the honor of meeting five Imams, except Jabir ibn Abdullah al-Ansari! What a blessing indeed!

As Jabir sat there, watching the young Imam (a), many thoughts raced through his mind. Maybe he sat there thinking, *oh, how blessed are those people who will live in the time of Imam al-Mahdi (AJ)! They will have the honor of being guided by the Imam (AJ) who will bring justice and peace to the entire world! I hope they will realize how blessed they are!*

That's us! Alhamdulillah, we are blessed to be living in the time of Imam al-Mahdi (AJ)! Oh, how lucky we are!

We pray that Allah hastens the reappearance of our awaited savior, Imam Muhammad al-Mahdi (AJ), who will guide us all to the right path. O Allah, please include us all among his true followers and help us pave the way for his return!

Biḥār ul-Anwār, Vol. 36, P. 250
Biḥār ul-Anwār, Vol. 52, P. 351
Kamāl ud-Dīn, Vol. 1, P. 146 & 365